W9-BIG-505

Book designed by
May Kramer-Muirhead

Illustrated by
Chris Riker

Copyright © 1985 by May Kramer-Muirhead

Illustrations copyright © 1985 by
Anro Communications

First printing 1985

Anro Communications
100 Tamal Plaza, Suite 108
Corte Madera, CA 94925

Library of Congress Cataloging in Publication Data

Burns, Robert, 1759–1796.
    The Best of Burns

    English and Scots.
    Includes index.
    1. Burns, Robert, 1759–1796—Translations, English.
I. Kramer-Muirhead, May, date. II. Title: The Best of Burns.
PR4304.E5K7   1985   821'.6   85–7371
ISBN 0–930623–01–0

Printed in the United States of America

This book presents

The Best of Burns

Robert Burns' Verses, Satires, Songs

———

Selected works translated by
May Kramer-Muirhead

Original text by
Robert Burns

ANRO COMMUNICATIONS, Corte Madera, California

Other books by May Kramer-Muirhead

Tam O'Shanter, A Scottish folk tale

Typesetting by
Publications Services of Marin
Novato, California
Production by Karol Wooley
Type styles Souvenir and Bookman

Dear Reader:

I have long felt the need for Robert Burns' works to be translated into modern English.

While admirers of this famous Scottish poet celebrate his 'immortal memory' once a year[1] and scholars continue to publish his work with the addition of their academic notes, the actual poems, epistles, satires and songs remain largely neglected. People in Scotland, never mind the rest of the world, have a difficult time reading the Lowland Scots period dialect in which Burns wrote.

This is a pity because Robert Burns wrote for enjoyment. Most people today do not even realise what a pithy and humorous writer he was.

Robert Burns—a ploughman to trade, a gifted writer by inspiration—has not only left us with amusing and enjoyable tales and poems; his work is an historical resource documenting the social, economic and religious conditions in which the rural people in Lowland Scotland lived before and after his time (1759–1796).

Burns is relevant to today's readers. The things that chiefly interested Burns—the human heart and human behaviour—have not changed. We can still laugh with Burns at the follies and foibles inherent in men and women.

May Kramer-Muirhead
San Anselmo, December, 1984

[1]Burns suppers are held throughout the world each year to celebrate his birthday—January 25th.

NOTE

These translations have been executed balancing the factors of accuracy, clarity of meaning and writing, and meter.

I have also taken the liberty, in this presentation, of deleting two verses from *Death and Doctor Hornbook,* excerpting lines from *Epistle to J. Lapraik* and abridging *The Cotter's Saturday Night.* This was an editorial decision.

M. K-M.

Contents

———

To a Mouse

On Turning Her Up in Her Nest, With
The Plough, November 1785

In this charming and spontaneous poem,
a ploughman shows his sensitivity towards a
mouse in particular and to the ecology of the field
in general. Burns' assertion that the best laid
schemes of mice and men are often overturned
by fate makes this poem a universal truth in a
minor key.

Wee, sleekit, cowrin, tim'rous beastie,
O, what a panic's in thy breastie!
Thou need na start awa sae hasty,
　　　　Wi' bickering brattle!
I wad be laith to rin an' chase thee,
　　　　Wi' murd'ring pattle!

I'm truly sorry Man's dominion
Has broken Nature's social union,
An' justifies that ill opinion,
　　　　Which makes thee startle,
At me, thy poor, earth-born companion,
　　　　An' fellow-mortal!

I doubt na, whyles, but thou may thieve;
What then? poor beastie, thou maun live!
A daimen icker in a thrave
　　　　'S a sma' request.
I'll get a blessin wi' the lave,
　　　　An' never miss't!

Thy wee-bit housie, too, in ruin!
Its silly wa's the win's are strewin!
An' naething, now, to big a new ane,
　　　　O' foggage green!
An' bleak December's winds ensuin,
　　　　Baith snell an' keen!

Wee, sleekit, cowering, timorous beastie
O what a panic's in your breastie
You need not start away so hasty
        With bickering prattle
I would be loathe to run and chase you
        With murdering rattle.

I'm truly sorry man's dominion
Has broken Nature's social union
And justifies that ill opinion
        Which makes you startle
At me; you poor earth-born companion
        And fellow mortal.

I'm sure that sometimes you may thieve
But then, poor beastie, you must live.
An ear of grain (or two at best)
        Is small request
I'll get the blessing of the rest;
        It won't be missed.

Your little house, too, is in ruin
Its silly walls the winds are strewing
You've nothing now to build a new one,
        Of mossy green,
And bleak December's winds ensuing
        Both fast and keen!

Thou saw the fields laid bare an' waste,
An' weary Winter comin fast,
An' cozie here, beneath the blast,
   Thou thought to dwell,
Till crash! the cruel coulter past
   Out thro' thy cell.

That wee-bit heap o' leaves an' stibble
Has cost thee monie a weary nibble!
Now thou's turn'd out, for a' thy trouble,
   But house or hald,
To thole the Winter's sleety dribble,
   An' cranreuch cauld!

But, Mousie, thou art no thy lane,
In proving foresight may be vain:
The best-laid schemes o' Mice an' Men
   Gang aft a-gley,
An' lea'e us nought but grief an' pain,
   For promis'd joy!

Still thou art blest, compar'd wi' me!
The present only toucheth thee:
But, Och! I backward cast my e'e
   On prospects drear!
An' forward, tho' I canna see,
   I guess an' fear!

You saw the fields laid bare and waste
And weary Winter coming fast
And cozy here, beneath the blast,
           You thought to dwell
Till crash! the cruel coulter[1] passed
           Out through your cell.

That wee bit heap of leaves and stubble
Has cost you many a weary nibble;
Now you're turned out, for all your trouble
           Of house and hall
To endure winter's sleety rain
           And frosty pall.

But Mousie you are not alone
In proving foresight may be vain.
The best laid schemes of mice and men
           Go oft awry
And leave us nought but grief and pain
           For promised joy!

Still you are blessed compared with me
The present only touches you
But o! I backward cast my eye
           On prospects drear
And forward, though I cannot see,
           I guess and fear.

[1]plough iron

Death and Doctor Hornbook

This tale is apparently based on a true story, but wildly exaggerated. The character of Hornbook is based on a John Wilson who, in addition to being a schoolmaster, had a grocer's shop where he added medicines to his stock and offered free advice on common complaints. Wilson is said to have boasted about his medical knowledge in the presence of Burns and thus inspired the story.

Burns has obviously enjoyed portraying the rascally apothecary of the tale in conflict with a character called Death and no doubt the victims who fell afoul of Hornbook are typical of the regional characters who crossed Burns' path.

Some books are lies frae end to end,
And some great lies were never penn'd:
Ev'n Ministers they hae been kenn'd,
        In holy rapture,
A rousing whid, at times, to vend,
        And nail't wi' Scripture.

But this that I am gaun to tell,
Which lately on a night befel,
Is just as true's the Deil's in hell
        Or Dublin city:
That e'er he nearer comes oursel
        'S a muckle pity.

The Clachan yill had made me canty,
I was na fou, but just had plenty;
I stacher'd whyles, but yet took tent ay
        To free the ditches;
An' hillocks, stanes, an' bushes kenn'd ay
        Frae ghaists an' witches.

The rising Moon began to glowr
The distant Cumnock hills out-owre:
To count her horns, wi' a' my pow'r
        I set mysel;
But whether she had three or four,
        I cou'd na tell.

Some books are lies from end to end
(And some great lies were never penned!)
Some ministers, they have been kenned
　　　　In holy rapture,
A rousing lie, at times, to vend
　　　　And nail with scripture.

But this that I am going to tell
Which lately on a night befell
Is true as ever the Deil's[1] in Hell
　　　　Or Dublin City;
That ever he comes near ourself
　　　　The more's the pity.

The village ale had made me cheery
I wasn't full, but only merry
I staggered some, but yet was wary
　　　　To clear the ditches,
Knew bushes, even in my hurry,
　　　　From ghosts or witches.

The rising moon began to hover
The distant Cumnock hills out over.
To count her horns, with all my power,
　　　　I set myself,
But whether she had three or four
　　　　I couldn't tell.

[1]The Devil

17

I was come round about the hill,
And todlin down on Willie's mill,
Setting my staff wi' a' my skill
  To keep me sicker;
Tho' leeward whyles, against my will,
  I took a bicker.

I there wi' Something does forgather,
That pat me in an eerie swither;
An awfu' scythe, out-owre ae shouther,
  Clear-dangling, hang;
A three-tae'd leister on the ither
  Lay, large an' lang.

Its stature seem'd lang Scotch ells twa,
The queerest shape that e'er I saw,
For fient a wame it had ava;
  And then its shanks,
They were as thin, as sharp an' sma'
  As cheeks o' branks.

'Guid-een,' quo' I; 'Friend! hae ye been mawin,
'When ither folk are busy sawin?'
It seem'd to mak a kind o' stan',
  But naething spak;
At length, says I, 'Friend, whare ye gaun,
  'Will ye go back?'

18

I had come round about the hill
And toddled down by Willie's mill
Setting my staff with all my skill
        To keep me steady,
But leeward, much against my will,
        Would sometimes eddy.

I then with *Something* did foregather
That put me in an eerie dither:
An awful scythe out o'er a shoulder
        Clear dangling hung;
A triple-pronged spear on the other
        Lay, large and long.

Its stature two Scotch ells,[1] I weened,
The queerest shape I ever dreamed
Its belly wasn't there, it seemed—
        And then its shanks
Were thin, and small, and sharp, and teamed
        Like matching planks.

"Good-eve," said I, "Have you been mowing
While other folk are busy sowing?"
It stood and looked at me with knowing
        But nothing spoke
At length said I: "Friend, where you going?
        Will you go back?"

[1] 6′6″ tall.

It spak right howe — 'My name is Death,
'But be na' fley'd.' — Quoth I, 'Guid faith,
'Ye're maybe come to stap my breath;
                    'But tent me, billie;
'I red ye weel, tak care o' skaith,
                    'See, there's a gully!'

'Gudeman,' quo' he, 'put up your whittle,
'I'm no design'd to try its mettle;
'But if I did, I wad be kittle
                    'To be mislear'd,
'I wad na mind it, no that spittle
                    'Out-owre my beard.'

'Weel, weel!' says I, 'a bargain be't;
'Come, gie's your hand, an' sae we're gree't:
We'll ease our shanks an' tak a seat,
                    'Come, gies your news;
'This while ye hae been mony a gate,
                    'At mony a house.'

'Ay, ay!' quo' he, an' shook his head,
'It's e'en a lang, lang time indeed
'Sin I began to nick the thread,
                    'An' choke the breath:
'Folk maun do something for their bread,
                    'An' sae maun Death.

It hollow spoke: "My name is Death
But don't be scared." Said I, "Good faith!
You're maybe come to stop my breath
   But hear me, lad
To harm you I would not be loathe
    See, here's a blade."

"Good man," said he, "put down your knife
I've no design to make you rife
I am inclined much less to strife
   Than mischief geared;
Mischief I like, but by my life,
    Don't spit my beard."

"Well, well," said I, "a bargain be it
Come, give your hand and we'll agree it
We'll ease our shanks and take a seat
   Come, what's your news?
These days you've been at many a meet
    At many a house."

"Aye, aye" said he, and shook his head
"It's been a long long time indeed
Since I began to nick the thread
   And choke the breath.
Folk must work hard to get their bread
    And so must Death."

Sax thousand years are near hand fled
'Sin' I was to the butching bred,
'An' mony a scheme in vain's been laid,
            'To stap or scar me;
'Till ane Hornbook's ta'en up the trade,
            'An' faith, he'll waur me.

'Ye ken Jock Hornbook i' the Clachan,
'Deil mak his king's-hood in a spleuchan!
'He's grown sae weel acquaint wi' Buchan,
            'An ither chaps,
'The weans haud out their fingers laughin,
            'An' pouk my hips.

'See, here's a scythe, an' there's a dart,
'They hae pierc'd mony a gallant heart;
'But Doctor Hornbook, wi' his art
            'And cursed skill,
'Has made them baith no worth a fart,
            'Damn'd haet they'll kill!

''Twas but yestreen, nae farther gaen,
'I threw a noble throw at ane;
'Wi' less, I'm sure, I've hundreds slain;
            'But deil-ma-care!
'It just play'd dirl on the bane,
            'But did nae mair.

"Six thousand years are nearly fled
Since I was to the killing bred
And many a scheme in vain's been laid
            To stop or nip me
'Till Hornbook's taken up the trade.
            I fear he'll whip me."

"You know Jock Hornbook down the hill?
(I wish the Deil[1] would take himsel'!)
He's studied Buchan[2] very well
            And other chaps
Now children laugh at me, not quail,
            And poke my hips."

"See, here's my scythe and there's my dart
They have pierced many a gallant heart
'Till Doctor Hornbook by his art
            And cursed skill
Has made them powerless to hurt.
            No one they'll kill!"

"When yesterday had just begun
I threw a noble throw with one
(With less, I'm sure, I've hundreds slain)
            But Devil care!
It just played rattle on the bone
            And did no more."

[1]The Devil
[2]Buchan's Domestic Medicine

'Hornbook was by, wi' ready art,
'An' had sae fortify'd the part
'That when I looked to my dart,
                'It was sae blunt,
'Fient haet o't wad hae pierc'd the heart
                'Of a kail-runt.

'I drew my scythe in sic a fury,
'I nearhand cowpit wi' my hurry,
'But yet the bauld Apothecary
                'Withstood the shock;
'I might as weel hae try'd a quarry
                'O' hard whin-rock.

'Ev'n them he canna get attended,
'Altho' their face he ne'er had kend it,
'Just shit in a kail-blade and send it,
                'As soon's he smells't.
'Baith their disease, and what will mend it,
                'At once he tells't.

'And then a' doctor's saws and whittles,
'Of a' dimensions, shapes, an' mettles,
'A' kinds o' boxes, mugs, an' bottles,
                'He's sure to hae;
'Their Latin names as fast he rattles
                'As A B C.

"Hornbook was by with ready art
And had so fortified the part
That when I looked upon my dart
 It was so blunt
It wouldn't even pierce the heart
 Of a kail-runt[1]."

"I drew my scythe in such a fury
(I almost tumbled with my hurry)
But yet the bold Apothecary
 Withstood the shock
I might as well have tried a quarry
 Of hardest rock."

"Even those he cannot self attend
People whose face he never kenned[2]
Defecate in a leaf and send
 To Hornbook here;
Then their disease and how to mend
 To Jock it's clear."

"And then a doctor's saws and whittles
Of all dimensions, shapes and mettles
All kinds of boxes, mugs and bottles
 He has, you see.
Their Latin names he rattles quick
 As A, B, C."

[1]cabbage stalk
[2]knew

25

'Calces o' fossils, earth, and trees;
'True Sal-marinum o' the seas;
'The Farina of beans and pease,
            'He has't in plenty;
'Aqua-fontis, what you please,
            'He can content ye.

'Forbye some new, uncommon weapons,
'Urinus Spiritus of capons;
'Or Mite-horn shavings, filings, scrapings,
            'Distill'd per se;
'Sal-alkali o' Midge-tail-Clippings,
            'And mony mae.'

'Whare I kill'd ane, a fair strae-death,
'By loss o' blood, or want o' breath,
'This night I'm free to tak my aith,
            'That Hornbook's skill
'Has clad a score i' their last claith,
            'By drap and pill.

"Calces of fossils, earth and trees,
True sal-marinum of the seas,
The farina of beans and peas,
          He has in plenty.
With aqua-fontis, what you please,
          He can content you."

"Except some new, uncommon weapons
Urinus spiritus of capons,
Or mite-horn shavings, filings, scrapings
          Distilled per se,
Sal-alkali of midge-tail clippings
          Et cet er a."

"Where I killed one, a fair bed death
By loss of blood, or want of breath
This night I'm free to take my oath
          That Hornbook's skill
Has clad a score in their last cloth
          By drop and pill."

'An honest Wabster to his trade,
'Whase wife's twa nieves were scarce weel-bred,
'Gat tippence-worth to mend her head,
             'When it was sair;
'The wife slade cannie to her bed,
             'But ne'er spak mair.

'A countra Laird had ta'en the batts,
'Or some curmurring in his guts,
'His only son for Hornbook sets,
             'An' pays him well.
'The lad, for twa guid gimmer-pets,
             'Was Laird himsel.

'A bonie lass, ye kend her name,
'Some ill-brewn drink had hov'd her wame;
'She trusts hersel, to hide the shame,
             'In Hornbook's care;
'Horn sent her aff to her lang hame,
             'To hide it here.

'That's just a swatch o' Hornbook's way,
'Thus goes he on from day to day,
'Thus does he poison, kill, an' slay,
             'An's weel paid for't;
'Yet stops me o' my lawfu' prey,
             'Wi' his damn'd dirt!

"An honest weaver to his trade
Whose wife's two fists were scarce well bred
Got tuppence-worth to mend her head
      When it was sore,
Then she slid quietly to her bed
      But spoke no more."

"A country laird was having fits
With something rumbling in his guts;
His only son Jock Hornbook gets
      And pays him well.
The lad for two good lamb-ewe pets
      'Came laird himself."

"A bonnie lass, you knew her name
Some ill-brewed drink had swelled her wame[1]
Trusted herself, to hide the shame,
      To Hornbook's care;
Horn sent her off to her long home
      To hide it there."

"That's just a swatch of Hornbook's way
Thus he goes on from day to day
Thus does he poison, kill and slay
      With foul concoctions
And cheats me of my lawful prey
      By all his actions."

[1]belly

'But hark! I'll tell you of a plot,
'Tho' dinna ye be speakin o't;
'I'll nail the self-conceited Sot,
            'As dead's a herrin:
'Niest time we meet, I'll wad a groat,
            'He gets his fairin!'

But just as he began to tell,
The auld kirk-hammer strak the bell
Some wee short hour ayont the twal,
            Which rais'd us baith:
I took the way that pleas'd mysel,
            And sae did Death.

"But listen, I'll tell of a plot
Though don't you go and speak of it!
I'll nail the self-conceited sot
         Like a dead herring
Next time we meet, I'll bet a lot,
          He'll get his fairing."

But just as he began to tell
The old church hammer struck the bell
Some wee short hour beyond of twelve
         Which roused us both.
I took the way that pleased myself
        And so did death.

Epistle to a Young Friend

Following the precepts of Scottish presbyterianism, Robert Burns attempted to be 'better' than he was. In industry and accomplishment, in self-educating himself far beyond his status in life, he succeeded admirably. However, he was unable to keep his physical appetites in check and this led to excesses on his part—in drink, in relations with women, and in being imprudent with money.

Robert Burns was no hypocrite. He regretted and criticised his own weaknesses and never lapsed into complacency or cynicism.

In writing this epistle (to young Andrew Aitken) Burns sets out the ideals that he believes in and there is sincere regret in the last lines which allude to the fact that he himself could not manage to live up to them.

I lang hae thought, my youthfu' friend,
    A Something to have sent you,
Tho' it should serve nae other end
    Than just a kind memento;
But how the subject-theme may gang,
    Let time and chance determine;
Perhaps, it may turn out a Sang;
    Perhaps, turn out a Sermon.

Ye'll try the world soon, my lad,
    And Andrew dear, believe me,
Ye'll find mankind an unco squad,
    And muckle they may grieve ye:
For care and trouble set your thought,
    Ev'n when your end's attainéd;
And a' your views may come to nought,
    Where ev'ry nerve is strainéd.

I'll no say men are villains a';
    The real, harden'd wicked,
Wha hae nae check but human law,
    Are to a few restricked:
But Och! mankind are unco weak,
    An' little to be trusted;
If Self the wavering balance shake,
    It's rarely right adjusted!

I long have thought, my youthful friend
A something to have sent you
Though it should serve no other end
Than just a kind memento.
But how the subject-theme may ring
Let time and chance determine
Perhaps it may turn out a song
Perhaps turn out a sermon.

You'll try the world soon, my lad
And Andrew dear, believe me
You'll find mankind a puzzling squad
And many times they'll grieve you.
For care and trouble set your thought
Even when your end's attainéd
And all your views may come to nought
Where every nerve is strainéd.

I'll not say men are villains all.
The really hard and wicked,
Who have no check but human law,
Are to a few restricted;
But oh! mankind are very weak
And little to be trusted
If you the wavering balance shake
It's rarely right adjusted!

Yet they wha fa' in Fortune's strife,
    Their fate we should na censure;
For still, th' important end of life
    They equally may answer:
A man may hae an honest heart,
    Tho' poortith hourly stare him;
A man may tak a neebor's part,
    Yet hae nae cash to spare him.

Ay free, aff han', your story tell,
    When wi' a bosom cronie;
But still keep something to yoursel
    Ye scarcely tell to onie:
Conceal yoursel as weel's ye can
    Frae critical dissection:
But keek thro' ev'ry other man
    Wi' sharpen'd, sly inspection.

The sacred lowe o' weel-plac'd love,
    Luxuriantly indulge it;
But never tempt th' illicit rove,
    Tho' naething should divulge it:
I waive the quantum o' the sin,
    The hazard of concealing;
But, och! it hardens a' within,
    And petrifies the feeling!

Yet they who fall in Fortune's strife
Their fate we should not censure;
For still, the important end of life
They equally may answer.
A man may have an honest heart
Though poverty hourly stare him
A man may take a neighbour's part
Yet have no cash to spare him!

So free, offhand, your story tell
When with a bosom crony
But still keep something to yourself
You scarcely tell to any.
Conceal yourself as well's you can
From critical dissection,
But look through every other man
With sharpened, sly inspection.

The sacred flame of well placed love
Luxuriantly indulge it
But never tempt the illicit rove
Though nothing should divulge it.
I waive the quantum of the sin
The hazard of concealing
But, oh! it hardens all within
And petrifies the feeling!

To catch Dame Fortune's golden smile,
    Assiduous wait upon her;
And gather gear by ev'ry wile
    That's justify'd by honour:
Not for to hide it in a hedge,
    Nor for a train-attendant;
But for the glorious privilege
    Of being independent.

The fear o' Hell's a hangman's whip
    To haud the wretch in order;
But where ye feel your honour grip,
    Let that ay be your border:
Its slightest touches, instant pause —
    Debar a' side-pretences;
And resolutely keep its laws,
    Uncaring consequences.

The great Creator to revere
    Must sure become the creature;
But still the preaching cant forbear,
    And ev'n the rigid feature:
Yet ne'er with wits profane to range
    Be complaisance extended;
An atheist-laugh's a poor exchange
    For Deity offended!

To catch Dame Fortune's golden smile
Assiduous wait upon her
And gather wealth by every wile
That's justified by honour;
Not for to hide it in a hedge
Nor for a train-attendant
But for the glorious privilege
Of being independent.

The fear of Hell's a hangman's whip
To hold the wretch in order
But where you feel your honour grip
Should always be your border;
Its slightest touches, instant pause—
Debar all side pretences—
And resolutely keep its laws
Uncaring consequences.

The great Creator to revere
Must sure become the creature,
But still the preaching cant forbear
And even the rigid feature;
Yet ne'er with wits profane to range
Be complaisance extended
An atheist-laugh's a poor exchange
For Deity offended!

When ranting round in Pleasure's ring,
    Religion may be blinded;
Or if she gie a random sting,
    It may be little minded;
But when on Life we're tempest-driv'n —
    A conscience but a canker —
A correspondence fix'd wi' Heav'n
    Is sure a noble anchor!

Adieu, dear, amiable youth!
    Your heart can ne'er be wanting!
May prudence, fortitude, and truth,
    Erect your brow undaunting!
In ploughman phrase, "God send you speed,"
    Still daily to grow wiser;
And may ye better reck the rede,
    Than ever did th' adviser!

When ranting round in pleasure's ring
Religion may be blinded
Or if she give a random sting
It may be little minded,
But when on Life we're tempest driv'n—
A conscience but a canker—
A correspondence fixed with Heav'n
Is sure a noble anchor!

Adieu, dear amiable youth!
Your heart never be wanting!
May prudence, fortitude, and truth
Erect your brow undaunting!
In ploughman phrase, "God send you speed,"
Still daily to grow wiser
And better may the advice heed
Than ever did the adviser!

Address to the Deil

The Deil[1] is a character who appears regularly
in Scottish folklore. Burns' Deil is the traditional
Scottish idea of the Devil—a wily, mischievous,
dangerous trickster also known as Auld Nick,
Hornie or Clootie. This Deil roams the countryside,
assuming animal or human form at will, and
frightens, seduces or harasses the country folk.
In Scottish religious teachings evil was no abstract
phenomena and the Devil was always at large just
waiting to snare the unwary.

It is typical of Burns that he can treat the
Devil with some compassion, pointing out that his
job is not exactly an enviable one, even for a devil.

[1]The Devil

O Thou! whatever title suit thee,
Auld Hornie, Satan, Nick, or Clootie,
Wha in you cavern grim an' sootie,
           Clos'd under hatches,
Spairges about the brunstane cootie,
           To scaud poor wretches!

Hear me, auld Hangie, for a wee
An' let poor, damned bodies be;
I'm sure sma' pleasure it can gie.
           Ev'n to a deil,
To skelp an' scaud poor dogs like me,
           An' hear us squeel!

Great is thy pow'r, an' great thy fame;
Far kend an' noted is thy name;
An' tho' yon lowin heugh's thy hame,
           Thou travels far;
An' faith! thou's neither lag nor lame,
           Nor blate nor scaur.

Whyles, ranging like roarin lion,
For prey, a' holes an' corners tryin;
Whyles, on the strong-wing'd Tempest flyin,
           Tirlin the kirks;
Whyles, in the human bosom pryin,
           Unseen thou lurks.

O You, whatever title suit you
Old Hornie, Satan, Nick or Clootie
Who, in that cavern grim and sooty
      Closed under hatches
Splashes 'round the brimstone cootie[1]
      To scald poor wretches.

Hear me, Old Hangie, for a wee
And let poor damned fellows be
I'm sure small pleasure it can be
      Even to a Deil[2]
To slap and scold poor dogs like me
      And hear us squeal.

Great is your power and great your fame,
Far known and noted is your name,
And though the flaming pit's your home
      You travel far;
You're not known to be slow or lame
      Nor loathe to scare.

While raging like a roaring lion
For prey, and holes and corners trying,
While on the strong-winged tempest flying
      To shake the kirk,
While in the human bosom prying
      Unseen you lurk.

[1]bowl
[2]Devil

I've heard my reverend Graunie say,
In lanely glens ye like to stray;
Or where auld, ruin'd castles, gray,
                    Nod to the moon,
Ye fright the nightly wand'rer's way,
                    Wi' eldritch croon.

When twilight did my Graunie summon,
To say her pray'rs, douce, honest woman!
Aft yont the dyke she's heard you bummin,
                    Wi' eerie drone;
Or, rustlin, thro' the boortries comin,
                    Wi' heavy groan.

Ae dreary, windy, winter night,
The stars shot down wi' sklentin light,
Wi' you, mysel, I gat a fright,
                    Ayont the lough;
Ye, like a rash-buss, stood in sight,
                    Wi' waving sugh.

The cudgel in my nieve did shake,
Each bristl'd hair stood like a stake,
When wi' an eldritch, stoor quaick, quaick,
                    Amang the springs,
Awa ye squatter'd like a drake,
                    On whistling wings.

I've heard my revered Granny say
In lonely glens you like to stray,
Or, where old ruined castles, gray,
      Nod to the moon
You fright the nightly wanderer's way
      With eerie croon.

When twilight did my Granny summon
To say her prayers (good, honest woman!)
Beyond the dyke she's heard you humming
      With eerie drone,
Or rustling through the elders; coming
      With heavy groan.

One dreary, windy, winter night
When stars shot down with slanting light
From you I got an awful fright
      The loch beyond.
You, like a rush bush, stood in sight
      And, waving, moaned.

The cudgel in my fist did shake
Each bristled hair rose like a stake
When with an eerie, hoarse, "quaick! quaick!"
      Among the springs
Away you scuttled like a drake
      On whistling wings.

Let warlocks grim, an' wither'd hags,
Tell how wi' you on ragweed nags,
They skim the muirs an' dizzy crags,
            Wi' wicked speed;
And in kirk-yards nenew their leagues,
            Owre howkit dead.

Thence, countra wives, wi' toil an' pain,
May plunge an' plunge the kirn in vain;
For, Oh! the yellow treasure's taen
            By witching skill;
An' dawtit, twal-pint Hawkie's gaen
            As yell's the Bill.

Thence, mystic knots mak great abuse,
On young Guidmen, fond, keen, an' crouse;
When the best wark-lume i' the house,
            By cantraip wit,
Is instant made no worth a louse,
            Just at the bit.

Let warlocks grim, and withered hags
Tell how, with you, on ragweed nags
They skim the moors and dizzy crags
       With wicked speed
And in church yards renew their leagues
       O'er dug-up dead.

Then, country wives, with toil and pain
May plunge and plunge the churn in vain
But no! the yellow treasure's gone
       By witching skill,
And petted twelve pint cow's become
       Dry as the bull.

Then knots appear from mystic cause
And confident young husbands rouse
When best of tools in all the house,
       By magic deed,
Are instant made not worth a louse
       When just in need.

When thowes dissolve the snawy hoord,
An' float the jinglin icy-boord,
Then, Water-kelpies haunt the foord,
            By your direction,
An' nighted Trav'llers are allur'd
            To their destruction.

An' aft your moss-traversing Spunkies
Decoy the wight that late an' drunk is:
The bleezin, curst, mischievous monkies
            Delude his eyes,
Till in some miry slough he sunk is,
            Ne'er mair to rise.

When Masons' mystic word an' grip,
In storms an' tempests raise you up,
Some cock or cat your rage maun stop,
            Or, strange to tell!
The youngest Brother ye wad whip
            Aff straught to hell.

Lang syne in Eden's bonie yard,
When youthfu' lovers first were pair'd,
An' all the Soul of Love they shar'd,
            The raptur'd hour,
Sweet on the fragrant, flow'ry swaird,
            In shady bow'r:

When thaws dissolved the snowy hoard
And float the icy surface board
Then water kelpies[1] haunt the ford
   By your direction
And sorry travellers are lured
   To their destruction.

And oft, a bog-traversing Spunk[2]
Decoys the chap that's late and drunk.
The nasty fellow, in a wink
   Deludes his eyes
'Till in some miry slough he's sunk
   No more to rise.

When mason's mystic word and grip
In storms and tempests rouse you up
Some cock or cat your rage must stop
   Or, strange to tell!
Your brother mason you would ship
   Straight off to hell!

Long past in Eden's bonnie yard
When youthful lovers first were paired
And all the soul of love; they shared
   The raptured hour
Sweet on the fragrant flowery swaird
   In shady bower.

[1]bog fairy
[2]spunkie; will-o'-the-wisp

Then you, ye auld, snick-drawing dog!
Ye cam to Paradise incog.
An' play'd on man a cursed brogue,
            (Black be your fa'!)
An' gied the infant warld a shog,
            'Maist ruin'd a'.

D'ye mind that day, when in a bizz,
Wi' reekit duds, an' reestit gizz,
Ye did present your smoutie phiz,
            'Mang better folk,
An' sklented on the man of Uzz
            Your spitefu' joke?

An' how ye gat him i' your thrall,
An' brak him out o' house an' hal',
While scabs an' botches did him gall,
            Wi' bitter claw,
An' lows'd his ill-tongu'd, wicked Scawl,
            Was warst ava?

But a' your doings to rehearse,
Your wily snares an' fechtin fierce,
Sin' that day Michael did you pierce,
            Down to this time,
Wad ding a Lallan tongue, or Erse,
            In prose or rhyme.

Then you, (old latch-releasing dog!)
You came to Paradise incog.
And deceived man, you wicked rogue
                    (Black be your fall!)
You gave the infant world a shock
                    'Most ruined all.

Remind that day, when in a buzz,
With smelly duds and bewigged pose
You did present your smutty phiz
                    To better folk?
And cast upon the man of Uzz[1]
Your spiteful joke?

And how you got him in your thrall
And broke him out of house and hall
While scabs and botches did him gall
                    With bitter claw?
Then you made loose his wicked scaul[2]
                    That's worst of all!

But all your doings to recite
Your wily snares and powerful might
Since that day Michael did you fight
                    Down to this time
Would beat a Lowland tongue, or Erse[3]
In prose or rhyme.

[1]Job, who symbolizes the age old suffering of the
  righteous man.
[2]scolding wife
[3]Irish gaelic

53

An' now, auld Cloots, I ken ye're thinkin,
A certain Bardie's rantin, drinkin,
Some luckless hour will send him linkin
                    To your black pit;
But, faith! he'll turn a corner jinkin,
                    An' cheat you yet.

But fare you weel, auld Nickie-ben!
O wad ye tak a thought an' men'!
Ye aiblins might — I dinna ken —
                    Still hae a stake —
I'm wae to think upo' you den,
                    Ev'n for your sake!

An now, Old Cloots, I know you're thinking
A certain Bard is ranting, drinking,
Some luckless hour will send him clinking
        To your black pit
But wait! He'll turn a corner winking
        And cheat you yet.

But fare-you-well, Old Nickie-ben
And would you take a thought on men?
Perhaps you might (I dinna ken)
        Still have a stake
I'm sad to think upon that den
        Even for your sake.

The Holy Fair

Scotland has long been renowned for the quality and training of its preachers, and this was also true in Burns' time. That is not to say that the religious speakers who preach at the Mauchline (Ayrshire) Holy Fair in this poem are typical of the breed. Burns is poking fun here not only at a religious 'fair' but at the foibles of the overly devout as well as the non-devout who flock to these affairs; on the one hand for entertainment and on the other for a religious scourging.

Upon a simmer Sunday morn,
　　When Nature's face is fair,
I walked forth to view the corn,
　　An' snuff the caller air.
The rising sun, owre Galston muirs,
　　Wi' glorious light was glintin;
The hares were hirplin down the furs,
　　The lav'rocks they were chantin
　　　　Fu' sweet that day.

As lightsomely I glowr'd abroad,
　　To see a scene sae gay,
Three Hizzies, early at the road,
　　Cam skelpin up the way.
Twa had manteeles o' dolefu' black,
　　But ane wi' lyart lining;
The third, that gaed a wee a-back,
　　Was in the fashion shining
　　　　Fu' gay that day,

The twa appear'd like sisters twin,
　　In feature, form, an' claes;
Their visage wither'd, lang an' thin,
　　An' sour as ony slaes:
The third cam up, hap-step-an'-lowp,
　　As light as ony lambie,
An' wi' a curchie low did stoop,
　　As soon as e'er she saw me,
　　　　Fu' kind that day.

58

Upon a summer Sunday morn
When Nature's face is fair
I walked forth to view the corn
And sniff the dewy air
The rising sun, o'er Galston moors
With glorious light was glinting
The hares were hopping down the fields
The laverocks they were chanting
                    Full sweet that day.

As lightsomely I gazed abroad
To see a scene so gay
Three lassies early at the road
Came hurrying up the way
Two had cloaks of doleful black
The other had grey lining
And she that walked a wee bit back
Was in the fashion shining
                    Full gay that day.

The two appeared like sisters, twin
In feature, form and clothes
Their faces withered, long and thin
Were sour as any sloes
The third came hopping, step and jump
As lightly as a lamb
And with a curtesy low did stoop
As up to me she came
                    Full kind that day.

Wi' bonnet aff, quoth I, 'Sweet lass,
  'I think ye seem to ken me;
'I'm sure I've seen that bonie face,
  'But yet I canna name ye.'
Quo' she, an' laughin as she spak,
  An' taks me by the hauns,
'Ye, for my sake, hae gi'en the feck
  'Of a' the ten commauns
        'A screed some day.

'My name is Fun — your cronie dear,
  'The nearest friend ye hae;
'An' this is Superstition here,
  'An' that's Hypocrisy.
'I'm gaun to Mauchline Holy Fair,
  'To spend an hour in daffin:
'Gin ye'll go there, yon runkl'd pair,
  'We will get famous laughin
        'At them this day.'

Quoth I, 'With a' my heart, I'll do't;
  'I'll get my Sunday's sark on,
'An' meet you on the holy spot;
  'Faith, we'se hae fine remarkin!'
Then I gaed hame at crowdie-time,
  An' soon I made me ready;
For roads were clad, frae side to side,
  Wi' monie a wearie body,
        In droves that day.

With bonnet off, said I "Sweet lass
I think you seem to ken me
I'm sure I've seen that bonnie face
But yet I cannot name you."
She told me, laughing as she spoke,
And holding both my hands,
"You, for my sake, have given the bulk
Of all the ten commands
           A rip some day."

"My name is Fun, your crony dear
The nearest friend you see
And this is Superstition here
And that's Hypocrisy
I'm going to Mauchline Holy Fair
To spend an hour in daffin
If you'll go there—that wrinkled pair—
We'll at them end up laughing
           Famously this day."

"With all my heart, I won't say 'nay'
I'll get my Sunday shirt on
And meet you on the holy way
We'll have some fine remarking!"
Then I went home at porrige time
And hurriedly got ready
For roads were clad from side to side
With many a weary body
           In droves that day.

Here, farmers gash, in ridin graith,
	Gaed hoddin by their cotters;
There, swankies young, in braw braid-claith,
	Are springin owre the gutters.
The lasses, skelpin barefit, thrang,
	In silks an' scarlets glitter;
Wi' sweet-milk cheese, in monie a whang,
	An' farls, bak'd wi' butter,
			Fu' crump that day.

When by the plate we set our nose,
	Weel heaped up wi' ha' pence,
A greedy glowr Black Bonnet throws,
	An' we maun draw our tippence.
Then in we go to see the show,
	On ev'ry side they're gath'rin;
Some carryin dails, some chairs an' stools,
	An' some are busy bleth'rin
			Right loud that day.

Here stands a shed to fend the show'rs,
	An' screen our countra Gentry,
There, racer Jess, an' twa-three whores,
	Are blinkin at the entry.
Here sits a raw o' tittlin jads,
	Wi' heaving breast an' bare neck;
An' there, a batch o' wabster lads,
	Blackguarding frae Kilmarnock
			For fun this day.

Here farmers shrewd in riding cloth
Went jogging past their cotters
There swankies young in good broad cloth
Are springing o'er the gutters
The lasses, hopping, barefoot throng
In silks and scarlet glitter
With sweet-milk cheeses brought along
And oatcakes baked with butter
             Full crisp that day.

The collection plate set 'neath our nose
Is well heaped up with half-pence
A greedy stare Black Bonnet throws
And we must pay our two-pence
Then in we go to see the show
On every side they're gathering
Some carry planks, some chairs and stools
And some are busy blethering
             Right loud that day.

An awning stands to fend the showers
And screen our country gentry
There, racer Jess, and two-three whores
Are blinking at the entry
Here sits a row of tittering jades
With heaving breasts and bare neck
And there a batch of weaver lads
Blackguarding from Kilmarnock
             For fun this day.

Here some are thinkin on their sins,
　　An' some upo' their claes;
Ane curses feet that fyl'd his shins,
　　Anither sighs an' prays:
On this hand sits a chosen swatch,
　　Wi' screw'd-up, grace-proud faces;
On that, a set o' Chaps, at watch,
　　Thrang winkin on the lasses
　　　　To chairs that day.

O happy is that man an' blest!
　　Nae wonder that it pride him!
Wha's ain dear lass, that he likes best,
　　Comes clinkin down beside him!
Wi' arm repos'd on the chair-back,
　　He sweetly does compose him;
Which, by degrees, slips round her neck,
　　An's loof upon her bosom
　　　　Unkend that day.

Now a' the congregation o'er
　　Is silent expectation;
For Moodie speels the holy door,
　　Wi' tidings o' damnation.
Should Hornie, as in ancient days,
　　'Mang sons o' God present him,
The vera sight o' Moodie's face,
　　To's ain het hame had sent him
　　　　Wi' fright that day.

Here some are thinking on their sins
And some upon their clothes
One curses feet that soiled his shins
Another sighs and prays
On this hand sits a chosen swatch
With screwed-up, grace-proud faces
On that, a set of chaps at watch,
Busy to wink the lasses
                    To chairs that day.

O happy is that man and blessed
(No wonder that it pride him)
Whose own dear lass, that he likes best,
Comes sitting down beside him.
With arm reposed on the chair-back
He sweetly does compose him
Which, by degrees, slips round her neck
And lights upon her bosom
                    Unknown that day.

Now all the congregation o'er
Is silent expectation
For Moodie climbs the holy door
With tidings of damnation
Should Hornie[1], as in ancient days
Among God's sons present him
The very sight of Moodie's face
Back home would straight have sent him
                    With fright that day.

[1]The Devil

Hear how he clears the points o' faith
    Wi' rattlin an' thumpin!
Now meekly calm, now wild in wrath,
    He's stampin, an' he's jumpin!
His lengthen'd chin, his turn'd-up snout,
    His eldritch squeel an' gestures,
O how they fire the heart devout,
    Like cantharidian plasters,
            On sic a day!

But hark! the tent has chang'd its voice;
    There's peace an' rest nae langer:
For a' the real judges rise,
    They canna sit for anger.
Smith opens out his cauld harangues,
    On practice and on morals;
An' aff the godly pour in thrangs,
    To gie the jars an' barrels
            A lift that day.

Hear how he clears the points of faith
With rattling and with thumping
Now meekly calm, now wild in wrath,
He's stamping and he's jumping
His lengthened chin, his turned-up snout,
Unearthly squeals and gestures
O how they fire the heart devout
Like cantharidian plasters
        On such a day!

But hark! the tent has changed its voice
There's peace and rest no longer
For all the real judges rise
They cannot sit for anger
Smith opens with his cold harangues
On practice and on morals
And off the godly pour in throngs
To give the jars and barrels
        A lift that day.

What signifies his barren shine,
     Of moral pow'rs an' reason?
His English style, an' gesture fine,
     Are a' clean out o' season.
Like Socrates or Antonine,
     Or some auld pagan Heathen,
The moral man he does define,
     But ne'er a word o' faith in
          That's right that day.

In guid time comes an antidote
     Against sic poison'd nostrum;
For Peebles, frae the water-fit,
     Ascends the holy rostrum:
See, up he's got the word o' God,
     An' meek an' mim has view'd it,
While Common-Sense has taen the road,
     An' aff, an' up the Cowgate
          Fast, fast that day.

Wee Miller niest, the Guard relieves,
     An' Orthodoxy raibles,
Tho' in his heart he weel believes,
     An' thinks it auld wives' fables:
But faith! the birkie wants a Manse,
     So, cannilie he hums them;
Altho' his carnal wit an' sense
     Like hafflins-wise o'ercomes him
          At times that day.

What signifies his barren shine
Of moral powers and reason?
His English style, and gesture fine
Are all clean out of season.
Like Socrates or Antonine,
Or some old pagan heathen,
The moral man he does define
But ne'er a word of faith in
                That's right this day.

In good time comes an antidote
Against such poisoned nostrum
For Peebles, from the water-foot
Ascends the holy rostrum;
See, up he's got the word of God
And meek and prim has viewed it
While common sense has taken the road
And off, and up the Cowgate
                Fast, fast that day.

Wee Miller next, the guard relieves,
And orthodoxy gabbles
Though in his heart he well believes
And thinks it old wives' fables;
But faith! the fellow wants a manse
So cannily he hums them
Although his carnal wit and sense
Nearly overcomes him
                At times that day.

Now, butt an' ben the Change-house fills,
    Wi' yill-caup Commentators:
Here's crying out for bakes an' gills,
    An' there the pint-stowp clatters;
While thick an' thrang, an' loud an' lang,
    Wi' Logic, an' wi' Scripture,
They raise a din, that, in the end,
    Is like to breed a rupture
        O' wrath that day.

Leeze me on Drink! it gies us mair
    Than either School or Colledge:
It kindles Wit, it waukens Lair,
    It pangs us fou o' Knowledge.
Be't whisky gill or penny wheep,
    Or ony stronger potion
It never fails, on drinkin deep,
    To kittle up our notion,
        By night or day.

The lads an' lasses, blythely bent
    To mind baith saul an' body,
Sit round the table, weel content,
    An' steer about the toddy.
On this ane's dress, an' that ane's leuk,
    They're makin observations;
While some are cozie i' the neuk,
    An' formin assignations
        To meet some day.

Now front and rear the tavern fills
With ale cup commentators,
Here's crying out for bakes and gills
And there the pint stowp clatters,
While thick and thrang and loud and long
With logic, and with scripture
They raise a din that, in the end,
Is like to breed a rupture
           Of wrath that day.

Drink's dear to me, it gives us more
Than either school or college
It kindles wit, it wakens lore,
It crams us full of knowledge
If whiskey gill or penny beer
Or any stronger potion
It never fails, on drinking cheer
To tickle up our notion
           By night or day.

Lads and lasses, in assent
To mind both soul and body,
Sit round the table, well content
And stir about the toddy
On this one's dress, and that one's look,
They're making observations
While some are cosy in the nook
And forming assignations
           To meet some day.

But now the Lord's ain trumpet touts,
    Till a' the hills are rairin,
An' echos back return the shouts;
    Black Russell is na spairin:
His piercing words, like Highlan swords,
    Divide the joints an' marrow;
His talk o' Hell, whare devils dwell,
    Our vera 'Sauls does harrow'[1]
        Wi' fright that day!

A vast, unbottom'd, boundless pit,
    Fill'd fou o' lowin brunstane,
Wha's ragin flame, an' scorchin heat,
    Wad melt the hardest whun-stane!
The half asleep start up wi' fear,
    An' think they hear it roarin,
When presently it does appear,
    'Twas but some neebor snorin
        Asleep that day.

'Twad be owre lang a tale to tell,
    How monie stories past,
And how they crouded to the yill,
    When they were a' dismist:
How drink gaed round, in cogs an' caups,
    Amang the furms an' benches;
An' cheese an' bread, frae women's laps,
    Was dealt about in lunches,
        An' dawds that day.

[1]Shakespeare's Hamlet.

72

But now the Lord's own trumpet sounds
Till all the hills are roaring
And echos back return the sounds;
Black Russell is not sparing.
His piercing words, like Highland swords
Divide the joints and marrow
His talk of Hell, where devils dwell,
Our very soul does harrow
              With fright that day!

A vast, unbottomed, boundless pit
Filled full of flaming brimstone
Whose raging flame, and scorching heat
Would melt the hardest whin-stone!
The half asleep start up with fear
And think they hear it roaring
When presently it does appear
'Twas but some neighbour snoring
              Asleep that day.

'Twould be o'er long a tale to tell
Of all the things that passed
And how folk crowded to the ale
When they were all dismissed;
How drink went round in cogs and cups
Among the forms and benches
And cheese and bread from women's laps
Was dealt about in lunches
              And lumps that day.

In comes a gaucie, gash Guidwife,
  An' sits down by the fire,
Syne draws her kebbuck an' her knife,
  The lasses they are shyer.
The auld Guidmen, about the grace,
  Frae side to side they bother,
Till some ane by his bonnet lays,
  An' gies them't, like a tether,
        Fu' lang that day.

Waesucks! for him that gets nae lass,
  Or lasses that hae naething!
Sma' need has he to say a grace,
  Or melvie his braw claithing!
O Wives be mindfu', ance yoursel
  How bonie lads ye wanted,
An' dinna, for a kebbuk-heel,
  Let lasses be affronted
        On sic a day!

Now Clinkumbell, wi' rattlin tow,
  Begins to jow an' croon;
Some swagger hame, the best they dow,
  Some wait the afternoon.
At slaps the billies halt a blink,
  Till lasses strip their shoon:
Wi' faith an' hope, an' love an' drink,
  They're a' in famous tune
        For crack that day.

In comes a jolly, shrewd goodwife
And sits down by the fire
Then draws her cheeses and her knife,
The lasses they are shyer.
The old goodmen, during the grace
From side to side make bother
'Till some one with his bonnet flays
And wields it like a tether
                  Full long that day.

Alas, for him that gets no lass
Or lasses that have nothing
Small need have they to say a grace
Or soil with food their clothing.
O wives, be mindful, once yourself
How bonnie lads you wanted
And do not for a wedge of cheese
Let lasses be affronted
                  On such a day.

Now Bellringer, with rattling rope,
Begins to ring the croon
Some swagger home (if they can cope!)
Some wait the afternoon.
At styles the fellows make a stop
While lasses strip their shoon[1]
With love and drink and faith and hope
They're all in famous tune
                  For talk that day.

[1]shoes

How monie hearts this day converts
    O' Sinners and o' Lasses!
Their hearts o' stane gin night are gane,
    As saft as ony flesh is.
There's some are fou o' love divine;
    There's some are fou o' brandy;
An' monie jobs that day begun,
    May end in Houghmagandie
        Some ither day.

How many hearts this day converts
Of sinners and of lasses
Their hearts of stone by night are gone
As soft as any flesh is.
There's some are full of love divine
There's some are full of brandy
And many jobs that day begun
May end in Houghmagandie
         Some other day.

Excerpt from

Epistle to J. Lapraik

    Robert Burns believed that his poetic talent
(which he modestly calls 'rhyming') derived from his
relationship with his Muse. In common with many
talented and creative writers (George Bernard Shaw
in a later period, for example) Burns did not have
a college education. Critics, it seems have college
educations and while Burns does not despise
education he points out that the acquisition of
a diploma does not an educated man make.

. . . . .

But, first an' foremost, I should tell,
Amaist as soon as I could spell,
I to the crambo-jingle fell.
        Tho' rude an' rough,
Yet crooning to a body's sel,
        Does weel eneugh.

I am nae Poet, in a sense,
But just a Rhymer, like, by chance,
An' hae to Learning nae pretence,
        Yet, what the matter?
Whene'er my Muse does on me glance,
        I jingle at her.

Your Critic-folk may cock their nose,
And say, 'How can you e'er propose,
'You wha ken hardly verse frae prose,
        'To make a sang?'
But, by your leaves, my learned foes,
        Ye're maybe wrang.

. . . . .

But, first and foremost, I should tell,
Almost as soon as I could spell
I to the rhyming-jingle fell,
        Though rude and rough,
Yet crooning only to myself
        Does well enough.

I am no poet, in a sense
But just a rhymer, like, by chance
And have to learning no pretence,
        Yet, what the matter?
When'er my Muse on me does glance
        I jingle at her.

Your critic folk may cock their nose
And say, "How can you e'er propose,
(Who hardly know a verse from prose)
        To make a song?"
But, by your leaves, my learned foes,
        You may be wrong.

What's a' your jargon o' your Schools,
Your Latin names for horns an' stools;
If honest Nature made you fools,
   What sairs your Grammars?
Ye'd better taen up spades and shools,
   Or knappin-hammers.

A set o' dull, conceited Hashes,
Confuse their brains in College-classes!
They gang in Stirks, and come out Asses,
   Plain truth to speak;
An' syne they think to climb Parnassus
   By dint o' Greek!

Gie me ae spark o' Nature's fire,
That's a' the learning I desire;
Then tho' I drudge thro' dub an' mire
   At pleugh or cart,
My Muse, tho' hamely in attire,
   May touch the heart.

     · · · · ·

What's all your jargon of your schools
Your Latin names for horns and stools;
If honest Nature made you fools,
          What serves your grammars?
You'd better take up spades and shools[1]
          Or workman's hammers.

A set of dull, conceited hashes
Confuse their brains in college classes
They go in steers and come out asses
          Plain truth to speak
And then they think to climb Parnassus
          By knowing Greek!

Give me one spark of Nature's fire
That's all the learning I desire
Then though I drudge through dub and mire
          At plough or cart
My Muse, though homely in attire
          May touch the heart.

. . . . .

[1]shovels

A Bard's Epitaph

Is there a whim-inspired fool,
Owre fast for thought, owre hot for rule,
Owre blate to seek, owre proud to snool,
   Let him draw near;
And owre this grassy heap sing dool,
   And drap a tear.

Is there a Bard of rustic song,
Who, noteless, steals the crowds among,
That weekly this area throng,
   O, pass not by!
But, with a frater-feeling strong,
   Here, heave a sigh.

Is there a man, whose judgment clear
Can others teach the course to steer,
Yet runs, himself, life's mad career,
   Wild as the wave;
Here pause — and, through the starting tear,
   Survey this grave.

The poor Inhabitant below
Was quick to learn and wise to know,
And keenly felt the friendly glow,
   And softer flame;
But thoughtless follies laid him low,
   And stain'd his name!

Reader, attend — whether thy soul
Soars fancy's flights beyond the pole,
Or darkling grubs this earthly hole,
   In low pursuit;
Know, prudent, cautious, self-controui
   Is Wisdom's root.

A Bard's Epitaph

Robert Burns was fond of writing epitaphs.
Here he writes what could have been his own.

Is there a whim inspired fool
Too fast for thought, too hot for rule?
Too shy to seek, to proud to crawl?
        Let him draw near;
And by this mound wax sorrowful
        And drop a tear.

Is there a Bard of rustic song
Who, noteless, steals the crowds among
That weekly this area throng?
        O, pass not by!
But with a frater-feeling strong,
        Here heave a sigh.

Is there a man whose judgement clear
Can others teach the course to steer
Yet runs, himself, life's mad career
        Wild as the wave?
Here pause—and through the starting tear
        Survey this grave.

The poor inhabitant below
Was quick to learn and wise to know
And keenly felt the friendly glow
        And softer flame;
But thoughtless follies laid him low,
        And stained his name!

Reader attend, whether your soul
Soars fancy's flights beyond the pole
Or darkling grubs this earthly hole
        In low pursuit;
Know prudent, cautious, self-control
        Is wisdom's root.

The Cotter's Saturday Night (abridged)

This poem is written mostly in English, after the style of Keats. Some people consider it to be Burns' finest poem. Others feel that it lacks the spontaneity and charm of his other works, written in the Lowland Scots dialect.

It is an important poem for several reasons. It gives us a picture, however idealised, of Scottish family life before industrialization. It illustrates very clearly what form religion took in Scotland and how deep and heartfelt were those beliefs. Most importantly, we see the other side of Robert Burns who so often attacked the hypocrisy inherent in religion. In this work he lauds true believers and morality. His Scottish patriotism also comes through in no uncertain terms.

My lov'd, my honor'd, much respected friend!
    No mercenary Bard his homage pays;
With honest pride, I scorn each selfish end,
    My dearest meed, a friend's esteem and praise:
To you I sing, in simple Scottish lays,
    The lowly train in life's sequester'd scene;
    The native feelings strong, the guileless ways,
What Aiken in a Cottage would have been;
Ah! tho' his worth unknown, far happier there,
        I ween!

November chill blaws loud wi' angry sugh;
    The short'ning winter-day is near a close;
The miry beasts retreating frae the pleugh;
    The black'ning trains o' craws to their repose;
    The toil-worn Cotter frae his labor goes,
This night his weekly moil is at an end,
    Collects his spades, his mattocks, and his hoes,
Hoping the morn in ease and rest to spend,
And weary, o'er the moor, his course does hameward
        bend.

At length his lonely cot appears in view,
    Beneath the shelter of an aged tree;
Th' expectant wee-things, toddlin, stacher through
    To meet their 'dad,' wi' flichterin' noise and glee.
    His wee bit ingle blinkin bonilie,
His clean hearth-stane, his thrifty wifie's smile,
    The lisping infant, prattling on his knee,
Does a' his weary kiaugh and care beguile,
And make him quite forget his labor and his toil.

My loved, my honoured, much respected friend!
No mercenary bard his homage pays;
With honest pride, I scorn each selfish end
My dearest wish, a friend's esteem and praise.
To you I sing, in simple Scottish lays,
The lowly train in life's sequestered scene,
The native feelings strong, the guileless ways,
What Aiken in a cottage would have been
And though his worth unknown, far happier there,
    I ween!

November chill blows loud with angry row
The shortening winter day is near a close
The miry beasts retreating from the plough
The blackening trains of crows to their repose.
The toil worn cotter from his labour goes.
This night his weekly moil is at an end,
Collects his spades, his mattocks and his hoes,
Hoping the morn in ease and rest to spend,
And weary, o'er the moor, his course does
    homeward bend.

At length his lonely cot appears in view
Beneath the shelter of an aged tree.
The hopeful wee ones run or totter through
To meet their dad, with fluttering noise and glee.
His wee bit ingle, blinking bonnily,
His clean hearth-stone, his thrifty wifie's smile,
The lisping infant, prattling on his knee,
Does all anxiety and cares beguile
And makes him quite forget his labour and
    his toil.

Belyve, the elder bairns come drappin in,
  At service out, amang the farmers roun';
Some ca' the pleugh, some herd, some tentie rin
  A cannie errand to a neibor town;
  Their eldest hope, their Jenny, woman-grown,
In youfu' bloom — love sparkling in her e'e —
  Comes hame; perhaps, to shew a braw
      new gown,
Or deposite her sair-won penny-fee
To help her parents dear, if they in hardship be.

With joy unfeign'd, brothers and sisters meet,
  And each for other's welfare kindly spiers:
The social hours, swift-wing'd, unnotic'd fleet;
  Each tells the uncos that he sees or hears.
  The parents partial eye their hopeful years;
Anticipation forward points the view;
  The mother, wi' her needle and her sheers,
Gars auld claes look amaist as weel's the new;
The father mixes a' wi' admonition due.

Their master's and their mistresses' command,
  The younkers a' are warned to obey;
And mind their labors wi' an eydent hand,
  And ne'er, tho' out o' sight, to jauk or play;
  'And O! be sure to fear the Lord alway,
And mind your duty, duly, morn and night;
  Lest in temptation's path ye gang astray,
Implore His counsel and assisting might:
They never sought in vain that sought the
      Lord aright!'

At last the older ones come dropping in.
At service out, among the farmers round
Some drive the plough, some herd, some
                    careful run
A heedful errand to a neighbour town.
Their eldest hope, their Jenny, woman grown,
In youthful bloom, love sparkling in her eye
Comes home; perhaps to show a new bought gown
Or share with them her hard-won penny fee
To help her parents dear, if they in hardship be.

With joy unfeigned, brothers and sisters meet
And each for other's welfare kindly cares
The social hours, swift-winged, unnoticed fleet
Each tells the strangest that he sees or hears
Anticipation forward points the view.
The mother, with her needle and her shears
Makes old clothes look almost as good as new.
The father mixes all with admonition due.

Their master's and their mistress's command
The young folk are all warned to obey
And do their labours with a careful hand
And not (though out of sight) idle or play
"And, O! be sure to fear the Lord alway
And mind your duty, duly, morn and night
Lest in temptation's path you go astray
Implore His counsel and assisting might
They never sought in vain that sought the
                    Lord aright!"

But hark! a rap comes gently to the door;
    Jenny, wha kens the meaning o' the same,
Tells how a neebor lad cam o'er the moor,
    To do some errands, and convoy her hame.
The wily Mother sees the conscious flame
Sparkle in Jenny's e'e, and flush her cheek,
    With heart-struck, anxious care, enquires
        his name,
While Jenny hafflins is afraid to speak;
Weel pleas'd the Mother hears, it's nae wild,
        worthless Rake.

With kindly welcome, Jenny brings him ben;
    A strappan youth, he takes the Mother's eye;
Blythe Jenny sees the visit's no ill taen;
    The Father cracks of horses, pleughs, and kye.
The Youngster's artless heart o'erflows wi' joy,
But blate and laithfu', scarce can weel behave;
    The Mother, wi' a woman's wiles, can spy
What makes the Youth sae bashfu' and sae grave;
Weel-pleas'd to think her bairn's respected like
        the lave.

O happy love! where love like this is found!
    O heart-felt raptures! bliss beyond compare!
I've paced much this weary, mortal round,
    And sage Experience bids me this declare —
'If Heaven a draught of heavenly pleasure spare,
'One cordial in this melancholy Vale,
    ''Tis when a youthful, loving, modest Pair,
'In other's arms, breathe out the tender tale,
'Beneath the milk-white thorn that scents the
        ev'ning gale.'

But hear! a rap comes gently to the door.
Jenny, who knows the meaning of the same
Tells how a neighbour lad came o'er the moor
To do some errands and convoy her home.
The wily mothers sees the conscious flame
Sparkle in Jenny's eye and flush her cheek
With heart struck anxious care, enquires his name
While Jenny is halfway afraid to speak;
Well pleased, the mother hear's it's no wild
        worthless rake.

With kindly welcome, Jenny brings him in
A strapping youth, he takes the mother's eye
Blythe Jenny sees the visit's well begun.
The father cracks of horses, ploughs, and kye[1]
The youngster's artless heart o'erflows with joy
But hesitant and shy can scarce behave
The mother, with a woman's wiles can spy
What makes the youth so bashful and so grave;
Well pleased to think her girl's respected like
        the lave[2]

O happy love, where love like this is found!
O heartfelt raptures, bliss beyond compare!
I've paced about this weary, mortal round
And sage experience bids me this declare :
"If Heaven a draught of heavenly pleasure spare,
One cordial in this melancholy vale,
It's when a youthful, loving, modest pair
In other's arms, breathe out the tender tale
Beneath the milk-white thorn that scents the
        evening gale."

[1]cattle
[2]rest

Is there, in human form, that bears a heart —
    A Wretch! a Villain! lost to love and truth!
That can, with studied, sly, ensnaring art,
    Betray sweet Jenny's unsuspecting youth?
    Curse on his perjur'd arts! dissembling smooth!
Are Honor, Virtue, Conscience, all exil'd?
    Is there no Pity, no relenting Ruth,
Points to the Parents fondling o'er their Child?
Then paints the ruin'd Maid, and their distraction wild!

But now the Supper crowns their simple board,
    The healsome Parritch, chief of Scotia's food:
The soupe their only Hawkie does afford,
    That 'yont the hallan snugly chows her cood:
    The Dame brings forth, in complimental mood,
To grace the lad, her weel-hain'd kebbuck, fell,
    And aft he's prest, and aft he ca's it guid;
The frugal Wifie, garrulous, will tell,
How 'twas a towmond auld, sin' Lint was i' the bell.

The chearfu' Supper done, wi' serious face,
    They, round the ingle, form a circle wide;
The Sire turns o'er, wi' patriarchal grace,
    The big ha'-Bible, ance his Father's pride:
    His bonnet rev'rently is laid aside,
His lyart haffets wearing thin and bare;
    Those strains that once did sweet in Zion glide,
He wales a portion with judicious care;
'And let us worship God!' he says, with solemn air.

Is there, in human form, that bears a heart
A wretch, a villain, lost to love and truth
That can, with studied, sly, ensnaring art
Betray sweet Jenny's unsuspecting youth?
Curse on his perjured arts, dissembling, smooth!
Are honour, virtue, conscience, all exiled?
Is there no pity, no relenting ruth
Points to the parents fondling o'er their child?
Then paints the ruined maid, and their distraction
          wild?

But now the supper crowns their simple board,
The wholesome porridge, chief of Scotia's food
And milk their only cow does them afford
(That snug partitioned off chews on her cud).
The dame brings forth, in complimental mood
To grace the lad, her long saved cheese as well
And oft he's pressed, and often calls it good
The frugal wife, garrulous, will tell
How 'twas a twelvemonth old, since flax was in
          the bell.

The cheerful supper done, with serious face
They, round the ingle, form a circle wide.
The sire turns over, with patriarchal grace
The big hall bible, once his father's pride;
His bonnet reverently is laid aside
His gray sidelocks are wearing thin and bare.
Those strains that once did sweet in Zion glide,
He names a portion with judicious care,
"And let us worship God!" he says, with
          solemn air.

Compar'd with this, how poor Religion's pride,
  In all the pomp of method, and of art,
When men display to congregations wide,
  Devotion's ev'ry grace, except the heart!
  The Power, incens'd, the Pageant will desert,
The pompous strain, the sacerdotal stole;
  But haply, in some Cottage far apart,
May hear, well-pleas'd, the language of the Soul;
And in His Book of Life the Inmates poor enroll.

Then homeward all take off their sev'ral way;
  The youngling Cottagers retire to rest:
The Parent-pair their secret homage pay,
  And proffer up to Heaven the warm request,
  That He who stills the raven's clam'rous nest,
And decks the lily fair in flow'ry pride,
  Would, in the way His Wisdom sees the best,
For them and for their little ones provide;
But chiefly, in their hearts with Grace divine preside.

Compared with this, how poor religion's pride
In all the pomp of method, and of art,
When men display to congregations wide
Devotion's every grace, except the heart!
The power, incensed, the pageant will desert
The pompous strain, the sacerdotal stole;
But maybe in some cottage far apart,
May hear, well-pleased, the language of the Soul
And in His Book of Life the inmates poor enroll.

Then homeward all take off their several way
The youngling cottagers retire to rest
The parent-pair their secret homage pay
And proffer up to Heaven the warm request:
That He who stills the raven's clamorous nest
And decks the lily fair in flowery pride,
Would, in the way His wisdom sees the best,
For them and for their little ones provide;
But chiefly, in their hearts with grace divine
preside.

O Scotia! my dear, my native soil!
  For whom my warmest wish to Heaven is sent!
Long may thy hardy sons of rustic toil
  Be blest with health, and peace, and sweet
  content!
  And, O! may Heaven their simple lives prevent
From Luxury's contagion, weak and vile!
  Then, howe'er crowns and coronets be rent,
A virtuous Populace may rise the while,
And stand a wall of fire around their much-lov'd Isle.

O Scotland! my dear, my native soil!
For whom my warmest wish to Heaven is sent!
Long may the hardy sons of rustic toil
Be blessed with health, and peace, and sweet
                    content!
And O! may Heaven their simple lives prevent
From luxury's contagion, weak and vile!
Then, however crowns and coronets be rent
A virtuous populace may rise the while
And stand a wall of fire around their much loved
                    isle.

Miscellaneous Burns

On Marriage

That hackney'd judge of human life,
The Preacher and the King,
Observes: — "The man that gets a wife
He gets a noble thing."
But how capricious are mankind,
Now loathing, now desirous!
We married men, how oft we find
The best of things will tire us!

On William Graham of Mossknowe

"Stop thief!" Dame Nature call'd to Death
As Willie drew his latest breath:
"How shall I make a fool again?
My choicest model thou hast taen."

On John Dove, Innkeeper
(Dove was the landlord of an inn in Mauchline)

Here lies Johnie Pigeon:
What was his religion
Whae'er desires to ken
To some other warl'
Maun follow the carl,
For here Johnie Pigeon had nane!

Strong ale was ablution;
Small beer, persecution;
A dram was memento mori;
But a full flowing bowl
Was the saving his soul,
And port was celestial glory!

Elegy On The Death Of Robert Ruisseaux

("Ruisseaux" is the French word for "brooks" which is a play on the word "burns").

Now Robin lies in his last lair,
He'll gabble rhyme, nor sing nae mair;
Could Poverty wi' hungry stare
        Nae mair shall fear him;
Nor anxious Fear, nor cankert Care,
        E'er mair come near him.

To tell the truth, they seldom fash'd him,
Except the moment that they crush'd him;
For sune as Chance or Fate had hush'd 'em,
        Tho' e'er sae short,
Then wi' a rhyme or sang he lash'd 'em,
        And thought it sport.

Tho' he was bred to kintra-wark,
And counted was baith wight and stark,
Yet that was never Robin's mark
        To mak a man;
But tell him, he was learned and clark,
        Ye roos'd him then!

On Tam The Chapman
(A Chapman is a peddler.)

As Tam the chapman on a day
Wi' Death forgather'd by the way,
Weel pleas'd he greets a wight so famous,
And Death was nae less pleas'd wi' Thomas,
Wha cheerfully lays down his pack,
And there blaws up a hearty crack,
His social, friendly, honest heart
Sae tickled Death, they could na part;
Sae, after viewing knives and garters,
Death takes him hame to gie him quarters.

For William Cruickshank, A.M.
(William Cruickshank, master of the Canongate High School in Edinburgh was later promoted to master of classics at the Edinburgh High School.)

Now honest William's gaen to Heaven,
I wat na gin 't can mend him:
The fauts he had in Latin lay,
For nane in English kent them.

For William Michie
(Schoolmater at Cleish Parish, Fifeshire)

Here lie Willie Michie's banes:
O Satan, when ye tak him
Gie him the schulin o' your weans,
For clever deils he'll mak them!

Songs

The Scottish people have always expressed themselves in song.

For his own pleasure, Burns collected songs. Scottish songs of the period often had two distinct parts—the lyrics, which had their title, and the air, or tune, which had its own title.

Burns would restore a song to its traditional air, write new words to a traditional tune, or take some of the existing songs and give them a more polished treatment. He also wrote many love songs.

He contributed songs to Johnson's Musical Museum and Thomson's Scottish airs, two of the most famous collections of Scottish songs which were being published during his lifetime, but would take no money for his work. It was a labour of love for him to help preserve the heritage of Scottish songs that we still enjoy, many of which are still being performed.

Ca' The Yowes to the Knowes

Ca' the yowes to the knowes,
Ca' them whaur the heather grows,
Ca' them whaur the burnie rowes,
   My bonie dearie.

Hark, the mavis' evening sang
Sounding Clouden's woods amang!
Then a faulding let us gang,
   My bonie dearie.
      Ca' the, etc.

We'll gae down by Clouden side,
Thro' the hazels spreading wide,
O'er the waves, that sweetly glide
   To the moon sae clearly.
      Ca' the, etc.

Yonder Clouden's silent towers,
Where at moonshine midnight hours,
O'er the dewy bending flowers,
   Fairies dance sae cheerie.
      Ca' the, etc.

There Was A Lad

There was a lad was born in Kyle,[1]
But what na day o' what na style
I doubt its hardly worth the while
    To be sae nice wi' Robin.

   Robin was a rovin' Boy,
      Rantin' rovin, rantin' rovin';
   Robin was a rovin' Boy,
      Rantin' rovin' Robin.

Our monarch's hindmost year but ane
Was five and twenty days begun,
'Twas then a blast o' Janwar Win'
    Blew hansel in on Robin.
     Robin was, etc.

The gossip keekit in his loof,
Quo' scho wha lives will see the proof,
This waly boy will be nae coof,
    I think we'll ca' him Robin.
     Robin was, etc.

He'll hae misfortunes great and sma',
But ay a heart aboon them a';
He'll be a credit 'till us a',
    We'll a' be proud o' Robin.
     Robin was, etc.

[1]a district in Ayrshire, Scottland.

John Anderson My Jo

John Anderson my jo,[1] John,
    When we were first acquent,
Your locks were like the raven,
    Your bonie brow was brent;
But now your brow is beld, John,
    Your locks are like the snaw,
But blessings on your frosty pow,
    John Anderson my jo.

John Anderson my jo, John,
    We clamb the hill thegither,
And monie a cantie day, John,
    We've had wi' ane anither:
Now we maun totter down, John,
    And hand in hand we'll go,
And sleep thegither at the foot,
    John Anderson my jo.

[1]sweetheart; darling

The Banks O' Doon

Ye Banks and braes o' bonie Doon,
   How can ye bloom sae fresh and fair;
How can ye chant, ye little birds,
   And I sae weary fu' o' care!
Thou'll break my heart thou warbling bird,
   That wantons thro' the flowering thorn:
Thou minds me o' departed joys,
   Departed never to return.

Oft hae I rov'd by bonie Doon,
   To see the rose and woodbine twine;
And ilka bird sang o' its luve,
   And fondly sae did I o' mine.
Wi' lightsome heart I pu'd a rose,
   Fu' sweet upon its thorny tree;
And my fause luver staw my rose,
   But, ah! he left the thorn wi' me.

O, Whistle An' I'll
Come to Ye, My Lad

CHORUS

O, whistle an' I'll come to ye, my lad,
O, whistle an' I'll come to ye, my lad,
Tho' father an' mother an' a' should gae mad,
O, whistle an' I'll come to ye, my lad.

But warily tent when ye come to court me,
And come nae unless the back-yett be a-jee;
Syne up the back-style, and let naebody see,
And come as ye were na comin to me,
And come as ye were na comin to me.
  O, whistle, etc.

At kirk, or at market, whene'er ye meet me,
Gang by me as tho' that ye car'd na a flie;
But steal me a blink o' your bonie black e'e,
Yet look as ye were na lookin at me,
Yet look as ye were na lookin at me.
  O, whistle, etc.

Ay vow and protest that ye care na for me,
And whyles ye may lightly my beauty a wee;
But court na anither, tho' jokin ye be,
For fear that she wyle your fancy frae me,
For fear that she wyle your fancy frae me.
  O, whistle, etc.

Green Grow the Rashes

Green grow the rashes, O;
Green grow the rashes, O'
The sweetest hours that e'er I spent
Were spent amang the lasses, O.

There's nought but care on ev'ry han',
    In ev'ry hour that passes, O:
What signifies the life o' man,
      An' 'twere na for the lasses, O.
        Green grow, etc.

The warl'y race may riches chase,
    An' riches still may fly them, O;
An' tho' at last they catch them fast,
      Their hearts can ne'er enjoy them, O.
        Green grow, etc.

But gie me a canny hour at e'en.
    My arms about my Dearie, O;
An' warl'y cares, an' warl'y men,
      May a' gae tapsalteerie, O!
        Green grow, etc.

For you sae douse, wha sneer at this,
    Ye're nought but senseless asses, O:
The wisest Man, the warl' e'er saw,
      He dearly lov'd the lasses, O.
        Green grow, etc.

Auld Nature swears, the lovely Dears
    Her noblest work she classes, O,
Her prentice han' she try'd on man,
      An' then she made the lasses, O.
        Green grow, etc.

Scots, Wha Hae

Scots, wha hae wi' Wallace bled,
Scots, wham Bruce has aften led;
Welcome to your gory bed,
        Or to victorie.

Now's the day, and now's the hour;
See the front o' battle lour;
See approach proud Edward's power —
        Chains and slaverie!

Wha will be a traitor-knave?
Wha can fill a coward's grave?
Wha sae base as be a slave?
        Let him turn and flee!

Wha for Scotland's king and law
Freedom's sword will strongly draw,
Free-man stand, or Free-man fa',
        Let him follow me!

By oppression's woes and pains!
By your sons in servile chains!
We will drain our dearest veins,
        But they shall be free!

Lay the proud usurpers low!
Tyrants fall in every foe!
Liberty's in every blow!
        Let us do, or die!

Auld Lang Syne

Should auld acquaintance be forgot
    And never brought to mind?
Should auld acquaintance be forgot,
    And auld lang syne!

    For auld lang syne, my jo,
        For auld lang syne,
    We'll tak a cup o' kindness yet
    For auld lang syne.

And surely ye'll be your pint stowp!
    And surely I'll be mine!
And we'll tak a cup o' kindness yet,
    For auld lang syne.
        For auld, etc.

We twa hae run about the braes,
    And pou'd the gowans fine;
But we've wander'd mony a weary fitt,
    Sin auld lang syne.
        For auld, etc.

We twa hae paidl'd in the burn,
    Frae morning sun till dine;
But seas between us braid hae roar'd,
    Sin auld lang syne.
        For auld, etc.

And there's a hand, my trusty fiere!
    And gie's a hand o' thine!
And we'll tak a right gude-willie-waught,
    For auld lang syne.
        For auld, etc.

A Red, Red Rose

O my Luve's like a red, red rose,
    That's newly sprung in June.
O my Luve's like the melodie
    That's sweetly play'd in tune.

As fair art thou, my bonie lass,
    So deep in luve am I;
And I will love thee still, my Dear,
    Till a' the seas gang dry.

Till a' the seas gang dry, my Dear,
    And the rocks melt wi' the sun:
I will love thee still, my Dear,
    While the sands o' life shall run:

And fare thee weel, my only Luve!
    And fare thee weel, a while!
And I will come again, my Luve,
    Tho' it ware ten thousand mile!

Glossary

a	all
acquent	acquainted
ae, ane	one
aff	off
agley	awry
aiblins	perhaps
ain	own
aith	oath
a-jee	ajar
amaist	almost
aqua-vitae	whiskey
auld	old
auld lang syne	the old days
ava	of all
a-wee	belittle
ay, aye	always
ayont	beyond
back-yett	back gate
baith	both
bane	bone
barefit	barefoot
bauld	bold
beld	bald
ben	through (into the . . .)
bicker	run; hurry
big	build
bill	bull
billies	fellows

birkie	fellow
bizz	bustle; buzz
black-bonnet	church elder
blate	shy; bashful
bleezin	blazing
blethering	chattering
bonie, bonnie	pretty; handsome
boord	surface
boortries	elder trees
braes	hills; slopes
braid	broad
braid-claith	broad-cloth
brattle	scamper
braw	pretty
brent	unwrinkled
brunstane	brimstone
butt and ben	kitchen and parlour
caller	fresh
canna	cannot
cannilie	carefully
canny; cannie	careful; quiet
cantraip	magic
cauld	cold
caup	cup
change house	tavern
Cheeks o'branks	wooden bridle
clachan	village
claes	clothes
claith	cloth
claithing	clothing
clark	a clerk; scholarly

114

Clootie	cloven-foot
coof	dolt
cootie	bowl
coulter	plough iron
countra	country
cowpit	fell; tumbled
crack	chat; conversation
cranreuch	hoar frost
cronie	intimate friend or companion
crouse	confident
crowdie	porridge; a dish made with sour milk
crump	crisp
curchie	curtsy
curmurring	rumbling
daffin	having fun; being silly
dails	planks
daimen icker	an occasional ear (of corn)
damn'd haet	damned who it (it wouldn't. . .)
dawds	lumps; large portions
dawtit	petted
ding	beat
dirl	rattle
douce, douse	sedate, serious, prudent
dow	can (am able)
dub	a puddle
eldritch	eerie; unearthly
Erse	Irish gaelic
eydent	diligent
fairin	desert

farls	small oat cakes
fash'd	bothered
faulding	folding
fause	false
fauts	faults
fechtin	fighting
feck	bulk
fell	pungent; deadly strong
fient a	not a . . . (Devil a . . .)
fient haet	the Devil have it (nothing have it)
fiere	comrade
flie	fly
fley'd	frightened; scared
flichterin	fluttering
foggage green	moss
forbye	besides
fou	full (drunk)
furs	furrows
gaen	gone
gane	gone
gang	go
gars	makes
gash	shrewd; wise
gate	road
gaucie	jolly
gaun	going
gear	goods; wealth
ghaists	ghosts
gie	give
gi'en	given

gimmer pets	pet ewes
gin	if
glowr'd	stared
graith	attire
gree't	agreed
guidmen	husbands
guidwife	wife; mistress of the house
gully	large knife
hae	have
haffets	side locks
hafflin	half; halfway
hald	holding
hallan	a partition
hame	home
hashes	oafs
haud	hold
haun	hand
hap	hop
het	hot
hirplin	hobbling
hizzies	young women; hussies
hoddin	a riding motion
hoord	hoard
howe	hollow
howkit	dug-up
hougmagandie	fornication
hov'd	swelled
ilka	every
ither	other
jauk	idle

jinkin	dodging
jo	sweetheart; darling
jow	ring
kail-blade	cabbage leaf
kail-runt	cabbage stalk
kebbuck	cheese
keekit	looked
kelpies	river demons or fairies
kend	known
kenn'd	knew
king's hood	stomach
kirk	church
kirn	churn
kittle	tickle
knappin	stone-breaking
knowes	hillocks; knolls
kye	cattle
lag	backward; slow
laith	loathe
laithfu'	sheepish
lair	learning
Lallan	lowland
lang	long
lang syne	long ago
lave	rest
leeze	dear is . . .
leister	fish spear
leuk	appearance; look
linkin	hurring
lint	flax

loof	palm
lough	lake
lour	loom
lowe	flame
lowin	flaming
lowing heugh	flaming pit
lows'd	loosed
lowp	jumped
lyart	grey
mae	more
mair	more
maun	must
mawin	mowing
melvie	soil
mim	prim; meek
mislear'd	mischevious
monie	many
muckle	much; great
nae, na	not, no
neebor	neighbour
neuk	corner
nick	cut
niest	next
nieve	fist
onie	any; anyone
out-owre	away over
pangs	crams; stuffs
paidl'd	paddled; waded

pattle	plough staff
penny-fee	wages
penny wheep	small beer
pleugh	plough
poortith	poverty
pouk	poke
ragwort	ragweed
raibles	gabbles
rairin	roaring
rantin	roistering
rashes	rushes
rass-buss	rush bush
reck the rede	take the advice
rede	advise
reekit	smelly; smoky
reestit gizz	scorched wig
rin	run
rowes	rolls
runkl'd	wrinkled
sae	so
saft	soft
sair	sore; aching
sairs	serves
sair-won	hard earned
saul	soul
sawin	sowing
scar	scare
scaud	slap; to scold
scaul; scawl	scold
scaur	scare

schulin	schooling
screed	rip; tear
shog	shake
shools	shovels
shouther	shoulder
sic	such
sicker	steady
simmer	summer
skaith	harm
skelping	hurrying
sklented	cast; slanted
sklentin	slanting
slaes	sloes
sleekit	sleek; sly
smoutie	smutty
snick	latch
snell	fast
stane	stone
stacher'd	staggered
stap	stop
stark	strong
stibble	stubble
stirks	steers
stoor	hoarse
strae	straw
strak	struck
straught	straight
sugh	cough
spak	spoke
spairges	splashes
spairin	sparing
speels	climbs

spunkie	will-o-the-wisp
spiers	asks
spleuchan	tobacco pouch
squatter'd	fluttered
swankies	strapping fellows; show offs
swither	doubt
syne	then
tae	to; toe
taks	takes
tent	care; heed
tentie	heedful; careful
thowes	thaws
thrang	busy; crowded
thrave	twenty four sheaves
tirlin	unroofing
tittlin	tittering
todlin	toddling
tow	rope
twa	two
twomond	twelve-month
unco	very
uncos	uncommon things
unkend	unknown
wabster	weaver
wad	would
wae	woe
waesucks!	alas!
wales	chooses
waly	robust

wame	belly
wark-lume	tool
warl'y	worldly
waukens	awakens
waur	worst
weans	children
weel	well
whang	large slice
wha	who
wham	whom
whittle	blade
whittles	knives
wight	fellow
whun-stane	whin-stone
whyles	sometimes
wyle	beguile
yell	dry
yill	ale
yont	beyond
younkers	youngsters
yowes	ewes

Index of Titles

Chris Riker is a graduate of AIS of Minneapolis in commercial art. She has studied fine art in college in Santa Rosa and won numerous awards and competitions. She exhibits in Northern California.

Chris was born in Eastland County, Texas.

She has been an illustrator for the last five years for the Navajo Mission in Flagstaff, Arizona, and has recently illustrated TAM O'SHANTER, A Scottish Folk Tale.

May Kramer-Muirhead was born and educated in Scotland. She has earned her living as a writer, editor and translator, working and residing in Toronto, New York, Amsterdam and San Francisco.

May has always been a Burns Scholar. She has dedicated much of her time of late to translating the works of Burns into modern English. She is committed to the idea that a writer of Burns' stature deserves to be read by contemporary readers.